The Life and Work of
Claude Monet

Sean Connolly

www.heinemann.co.uk/library
Visit our website to find out more information about **Heinemann Library** books.

To order:
☎ Phone 44 (0) 1865 888066
🖹 Send a fax to 44 (0) 1865 314091
💻 Visit the Heinemann Bookshop at www.heinemann.co.uk/library to browse our catalogue and order online.

First published in Great Britain by Heinemann Library, Halley Court, Jordan Hill, Oxford OX2 8EJ, part of Harcourt Education.
Heinemann is a registered trademark of Harcourt Education Ltd.

Editorial: Clare Lewis
Design: Jo Hinton-Malivoire and Q2A Creative
Illustrations by Fiona Osbaldstone
Production: Helen McCreath

Printed and bound in China by South China Printing Company

10 digit ISBN 0 431 09881 6
13 digit ISBN 978 0 431 09881 4

10 09 08 07 06
10 9 8 7 6 5 4 3 2 1

British Library Cataloguing in Publication Data
Conolly, Sean
The Life and Work of: Claude Monet - 2nd edition
759.4
A full catalogue record for this book is available from the British Library.

Acknowledgements
The publishers would like to thank the following for permission to reproduce photographs:
Page 4, Portrait photograph of Claude Monet in front of the pictures Waterlilies in his studio. Page 5, Claude Monet *The Waterlilies - The Clouds*, Credit: The Bridgeman Art Library/Giraudon. Page 6, *Le Harve*, Credit: Bibliotheque Nationale. Page 7, Claude Monet *The coast of Normandy viewed from Sainte-Adresse*, Credit: The Fine Arts Museum of San Francisco. Page 9, Claude Monet *Caricature of a young dandy with a monocle*, Credit: Giraudon. Page 11, *Claude Monet Le Pave de Chailly*, Credit: Giraudon. Page 12, National Gallery, London, Credit: Hulton Getty. Page 13, Claude Monet *The Thames below Westminster*, Credit: The Bridgeman Art Library/National Gallery. Page 14, Edouard Manet *Monet in his studio*, Credit: AKG. Page 15, Claude Monet *Boulevard St Denis, Argenteuil, in Winter*, Credit: Richard Saltonstall/Museum of Fine Arts, Boston. Page 16, *Boulevard des Capucines*, Credit: Hulton Getty. Page 17, Claude Monet *Impression, Sunrise*, Credit: Giraudon. Page 19, Claude Monet *Entrance to the Village of Vetheuil*, Credit: Exley/Rosenthal. Page 21, Claude Monet *Haystack at Giverny*, Credit: The Bridgeman Art Library/ Hermitage. Page 23, Claude Monet *The Cap of Antibes, Mistral*, Credit: AKG. Page 24, Rouen Cathedral, Credit: Pix. Page 25, Claude Monet *Rouen Cathedral, Albany Tower, Early Morning*, Credit: Exley/Rosenthal. Page 26, Portrait photograph of Claude Monet and his wife Alice, St Mark's Square, Venice, Credit: Giraudon. Page 27, Claude Monet *Palazzo de Mula, Venice*, Credit: Exley/Rosenthal. Page 28, Photograph of Monet in his garden, Credit: Corbis. Page 29, Claude Monet *Waterlilies*, Credit: Giraudon.

Cover photograph: *Poppy field in a hollow near Giverny* by Claude Monet, reproduced with permission of Museum of Fine Arts, Boston, Massachusetts, USA, Juliana Cheney Edwards Collection.

The publishers would like to thank Nancy Harris for her assistance in the preparation of this book.

Every effort has been made to contact copyright holders of any material reproduced in this book. Any omissions will be rectified in subsequent printings if notice is given to the publishers.

The paper used to print this book comes from sustainable resources.

Some words in the book are bold, **like this**. You can find out what they mean by looking in the Glossary.

Contents

Who was Claude Monet?

Claude Monet was a French artist. He was one of the **Impressionists**. This group of painters tried to show how light changed through the day in their paintings.

Claude painted the same **scene** many times to show the change of light. This painting shows clouds **reflected** in the lily pond in his garden.

Early years

Claude Oscar Monet was born in Paris, France, on 14 November 1840. His family soon moved to the **port** of Le Havre. Claude liked being near the sea.

Claude loved the way light showed on
water. This drawing shows the coast near
Le Havre. Claude drew the picture when
he was 24 years old.

Schoolboy success

Claude did not like school. He made clever drawings of his classmates. A local painter called Eugène Boudin saw these drawings. He wanted Claude to become a painter.

Claude could pick out the important bits to draw. He was 16 years old when he made this funny drawing of a young man dressed in stylish clothes.

Making friends

In 1861 Claude joined the army but became ill after a year. His family gave him some money to become a painter. Claude moved to Paris when he was 22 years old.

Claude became close friends with other young artists in Paris. They often painted together. Claude painted this **scene** on a trip to the countryside near Paris.

Living in London

In 1870 Claude married Camille Doncieux. France was at war with Germany. Paris was dangerous so Claude and his wife moved to London. This is a picture of how London looked then.

Claude and his wife lived for a while
in London. Claude saw many paintings
by English artists. He painted the River
Thames many times while he was
in London.

Discovering light

In 1871 Claude moved to Argenteuil, a small town near Paris. He built a floating **studio** to **study** how light affects water. This is a picture of Claude painting in his studio.

Claude liked to paint outside in every season. This painting shows a street in Argenteuil in the winter. He painted it in 1875.

Impressionism

Claude and his friends painted quickly. Most **galleries** thought their paintings looked messy. In 1874 the group **exhibited** their own paintings. The exhibition was in a building in this street.

The group became known as the **Impressionists**. The name came from the title of this painting by Claude called *Impression, Sunrise*. It shows a harbour just after **dawn**.

Two families

Claude and his family moved to a town called Vétheuil. They moved in with their friend Alice Hoschede and her children. Claude now had to look after two families and eight children.

Claude began painting around his new
home in Vétheuil. He used quick **strokes**
of the brush to show light and shape.

Giverny

In 1879 Claude's wife Camille died. In 1883 Claude and the two families moved to Giverny, near Paris. He loved his new garden. He also painted in the countryside.

Claude worked quickly. He began painting the same **scenes** over and over. This painting tells us about the houses, fields, and even the weather in one afternoon.

Painting trips

Claude spent many months away from home each year during the 1880s. He travelled around France and painted many **landscapes**. He worked in all sorts of weather.

This painting shows the seashore in the south of France. Claude used quick **brushwork**. We can almost feel the wind blowing through the trees and across the sea.

Series paintings

Claude kept painting the same **scenes** at different times. Together these pictures are known as his **series paintings**. He painted this **cathedral** at Rouen many times.

Claude loved to paint the front of Rouen Cathedral. It is almost hidden by mist in this picture. Other paintings show it in bright sunshine.

Travels

Claude made his last painting trips when he was over 60 years old. He went to Spain, Holland, England, and Italy. This is a picture of Claude and Alice in Venice, Italy.

Claude loved the buildings in Venice.
They rise straight out of the water.
This painting shows a beautiful palace
reflected in the water.

Water lilies

Claude spent his last years at home in Giverny. He still thought about light and shape. He died on 5 December 1926. He was 86 years old.

Many of Claude's last works were huge paintings of water lilies. In this painting it is hard to tell where the lilies end and their **reflections** begin.

Timeline

1840   Claude Monet is born in Paris on 14 November, but soon moves to Le Havre.

1857   Claude meets the painter Eugène Boudin.

1862   Claude moves to Paris to become a painter.

1865–66   Claude has paintings shown to the public in Paris.

1870   Claude marries Camille Doncieux and lives in London.

1870–71   War between France and Germany.

1871   Claude moves to a new house in Argenteuil.

1874   Claude helps set up the first **exhibition** by the **Impressionists**.

1879   Camille dies. The artist Paul Klee is born in Switzerland.

1883   Claude moves to Giverny.

1893   Claude begins work on building a pond in the garden at Giverny.

1909   First public showing of Claude's water lily paintings.

1912   Claude develops an eye illness which slows his painting.

1926   Claude Monet dies on 5 December.

Glossary

brushwork marks left by an artist's paint brush

cathedral large church

dawn when it starts to get light in the morning

exhibit display works of art

gallery place where works of art are shown and sold

Impressionists group of artists who painted freely, showing light and movement

landscape painting of the countryside

port city on the edge of the ocean

reflect give a second picture of something, as with a mirror

scene place or area

series paintings many paintings of the same subject but painted at different times

stroke mark made by one movement of the brush

studio special room or building where an artist works

study to learn about a subject

More books to read

Masterpieces: Monet, Shelly Swanson Sateren (Franklin Watts, 2004)

The Children's Book of Art, Rosie Dickens (Usborne Publishing, 2005)

More paintings to see

Poplars, Claude Monet, The Fitzwilliam Museum, Cambridge

Rouen Cathedral Façade, Claude Monet, National Museum of Wales, Cardiff

The Water Lily Pond, Claude Monet, National Gallery, London

Index